FLOWERS

COLORING BOOK

BY JULIAN BAUM

CHP

COAL HARBOUR PUBLISHING

THIS BOOK

BELONGS TO

_____

Flowers. Coloring Book

Book Copyright © 2018 by Coal Harbour Publishing Ltd.

125A-1030 Denman St. Vancouver,

British Columbia, V6G 2M6, Canada

www.coalharbourpublishing.com

Publication Data

_____

Author: Baum, Julian

Title: Flowers. Coloring Book/Baum, Julian--1st ed.

Publication date: August 2018

Publisher: Coal Harbour Publishing Ltd.

Cover design © 2018 Coal Harbour Publishing

ISBN 978-1-989043-18-9 (Paperback)

CHP

FLOWER COLORING TIPS!

To color the drawings, you may use crayons or different types of markers. To obtain the best outcome though, it is highly recommended that you use alcohol-based markers.

Julian Baum

Julian Baum

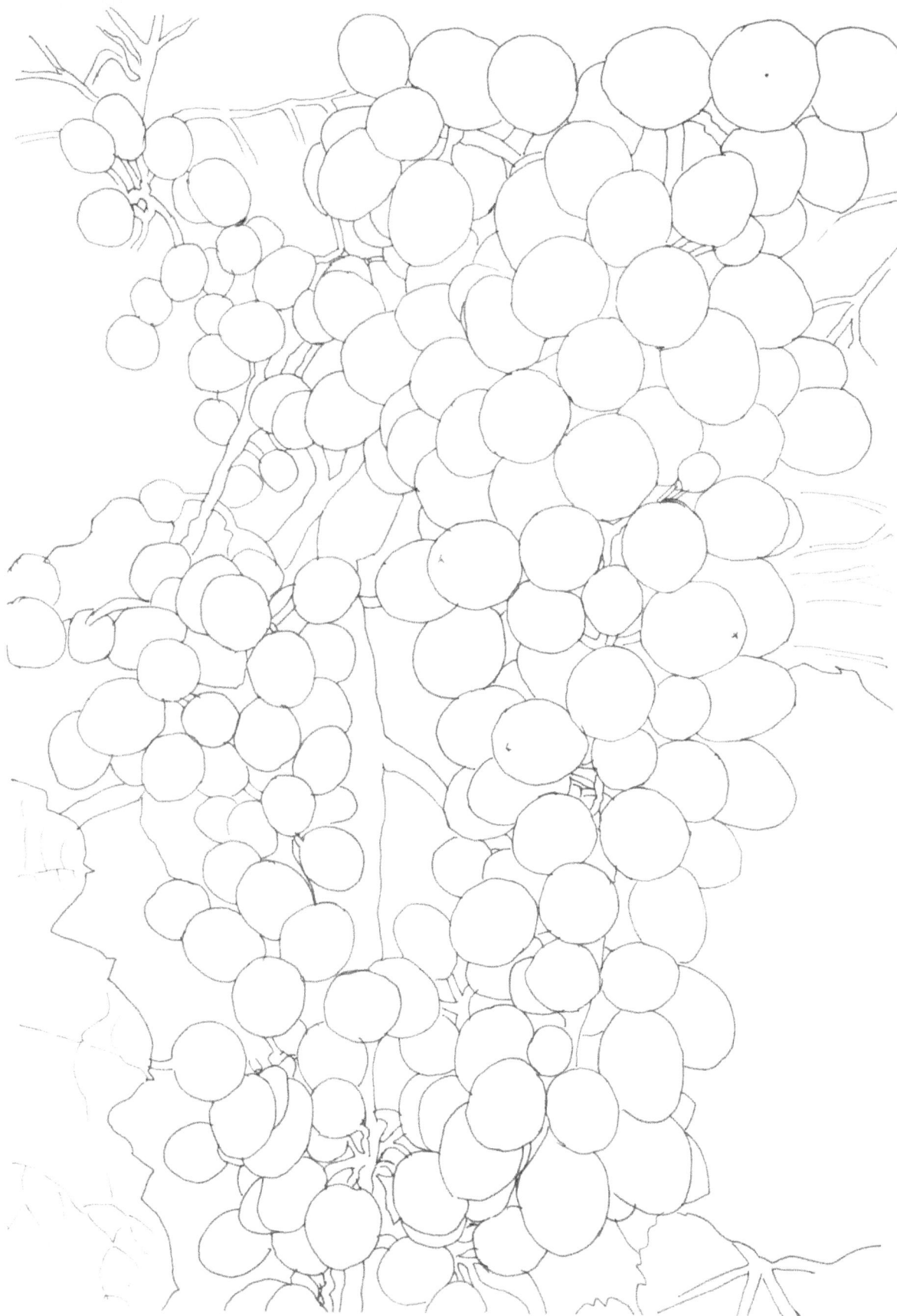

Julian Baum

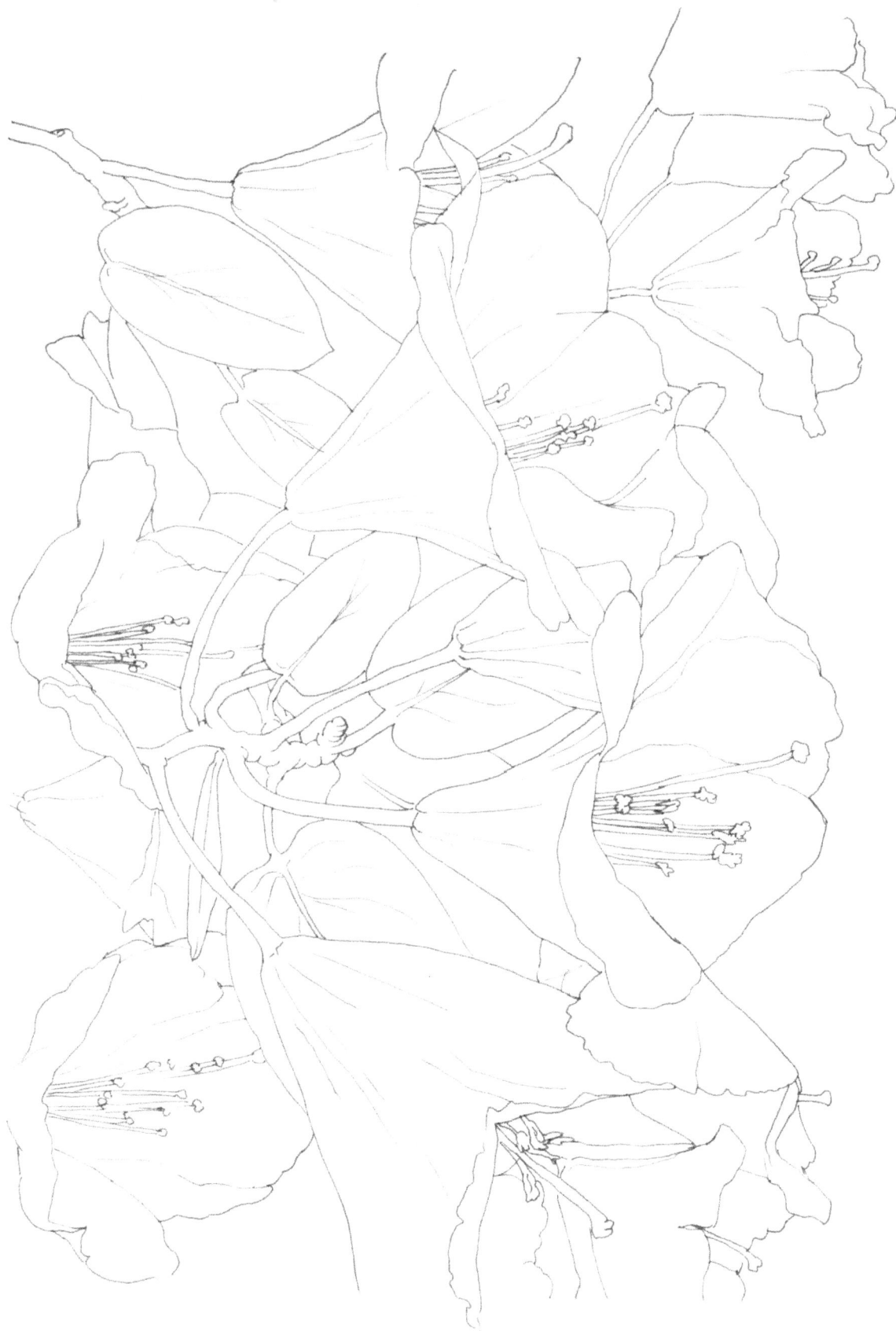

MORE COLORING BOOKS BY JULIAN BAUM

For detailed information, please visit the publisher's website

www.coalharbourpublishing.com